# SHAKESPEARE IN LOVE

## THE LOVE POETRY OF WILLIAM SHAKESPEARE

# Shakespeare In Love

## The Love Poetry Of William Shakespeare

*faber and faber*

The Love Poetry of William Shakespeare
First published in the United States in 1998
by Miramax Books/Hyperion

First published in the United Kingdom in 1999
by Faber and Faber Limited
3 Queen Square London WC1N 3AU

Published by arrangement with Hyperion, 114 Fifth Avenue,
New York, New York 10011, U.S.A

Printed in Great Britain by Bath Press Colourbooks, Glasgow

Compilation © 1998 Miramax Books/Hyperion
Photography © 1998, Miramax Films
Photographs by Laurie Sparham and Nigel Parry
Shakespeare in Love screenplay excerpts © 1998,
Marc Norman and Tom Stoppard

A CIP record for this book
is available from the British Library

ISBN 0-571-20093-1

4 6 8 10 9 7 5 3

# ❧ Table Of Contents ❧

## ❧ Plays ❧

## ❧ Songs ❧

## ⤜ Sonnets ⤛

WARWICKE

Parte of
Stafford
shire

THE COUNTI of
WARWICK
THE SHIRE TOWNE
AND CITIE OF CO:
VENTRE described

PART OF WOR:
CES TER

OCCIDENS

Anno Domini 1610.

THE SCALE OF MILES

Performed by Iohn Speede, And are
to be sold in Popes-heade ally against
the Exchange by Iohn Sudbury, and
George Humble.
Cum Privilegio.

A SCALE OF MILES

Gloucester Shire

HEMLINFORD

Solihull

PART OF
KINETON HUND

BARLICHWAYE HUNDRED
Henley in Arde

Aulcester

Feckenham
Forest

SHIRE

Parte
of
TER
SHIRE
shipston

Campden

PART OF
WORCES: part OF GLOSTER

Sutton Cofeld

Bermicham

CExOVENTREE

PART OF

LEICES TER SHIRE

THE LIBERTY OF COVENTRE

COVENTRE

KNIGHTLOW HUNDR.

Rugby

PARTE OF

NORTH AMPTON SHIR

KYNETON HUNDRED

Kyneton

Parte of

PART OF GLOCESTER SHIRE

Banbury

Oxford Shire

Jodocus Hondius excudit.

THE ARMES
OF SUCH HONORA
BLE FAMYLIES AS
HAVE BENE EARLS
OF WARWICK

Henry of Nuburgh | John Marshall | John de Plesseis

William Malduit | William Beauchamp | John Holland

Richard Nevill | George D. of Clarence | John Dudley

At Wolney in this Countye King Edward 4. ga-
thering his forces to recover his former losse,
was suddenly surprised and taken prisoner by his
brother George Duke of Clarence and Richard ...
the Stout Earle of Warwick and thence con-
veyed to the castell of Midleham in Yorkshire
whence shortly he escaped and came to London,
Anno Domini 1469.

I will have poetry in my life. And adventure. And love. Love above all. No…not the artful postures of love, not playful and poetical games of love for the amusement of an evening, but love that…over-throws life. Unbiddable, ungovernable—like a riot in the heart, and nothing to be done, come ruin or rapture. Love—like there has never been in a play.

*Shakespeare in Love* Screenplay
by Marc Norman and Tom Stoppard

I would stay asleep
my whole life if
I could dream
myself into a
company of
players.

*Shakespeare in Love*

# Shakespeare's
# Plays

Love is a smoke made with the fume of sighs;
Being purg'd, a fire sparkling in lovers' eyes;
Being vex'd, a sea nourish'd with lovers' tears;
What is it else? A madness most discreet,
A choking gall, and a preserving sweet.

*Romeo and Juliet* (I.i)

*O*, she doth teach the torches to burn bright!
Her beauty hangs upon the cheek of night
Like a rich jewel in an Ethiop's ear;
Beauty too rich for use, for earth too dear!
So shows a snowy dove trooping with crows,
As yonder lady o'er her fellows shows.
The measure done, I'll watch her place of stand,
And, touching hers, make blessed my rude hand.
Did my heart love till now? Forswear it, sight!
For I ne'er saw true beauty till this night.

*Romeo and Juliet* (I.v)

But soft! What light through yonder window breaks?

It is the East, and Juliet is the sun!

Arise, fair sun, and kill the envious moon,

Who is already sick and pale with grief

That thou her maid art far more fair than she.

Be not her maid, since she is envious.

Her vestal livery is but sick and green,

And none but fools do wear it. Cast it off.

It is my lady; O, it is my love!

O that she knew she were!

She speaks, yet she says nothing. What of that?

Her eye discourses; I will answer it.

I am too bold, 'tis not to me she speaks.

Two of the fairest stars in all the heaven,

Having some business, do entreat her eyes

To twinkle in their spheres till they return.

What if her eyes were there, they in her head?

The brightness of her cheek would shame those stars

As daylight doth a lamp; her eyes in heaven

Would through the airy region stream so bright

That birds would sing and think it were not night.

See how she leans her cheek upon her hand!

O that I were a glove upon that hand,

That I might touch that cheek!

*Romeo and Juliet* (II.ii)

'Tis but thy name that is my enemy:
Thou art thyself, though not a Montague.
What's Montague? It is nor hand nor foot
Nor arm nor face nor any other part
Belonging to a man. O be some other name.
What's in a name? That which we call a rose
By any other word would smell as sweet;
So Romeo would, were he not Romeo call'd,
Retain that dear perfection which he owes
Without that title. Romeo, doff thy name
And for thy name, which is no part of thee,
Take all myself.

*Romeo and Juliet* (II.ii)

Gallop apace, you fiery-footed steeds,
Towards Phoebus' lodging! Such a waggoner
As Phaeton would whip you to the west
And bring in cloudy night immediately.
Spread thy close curtain, love-performing night,
That runaway's eyes may wink, and Romeo
Leap to these arms untalked of and unseen.
Lovers can see to do their amorous rites
By their own beauties; or, if love be blind,
It best agrees with night. Come, civil night,
Thou sober suited matron, all in black,
And learn me how to lose a winning match
Played for a pair of stainless maidenhoods.
Hood my unmanned blood, bating in my cheeks,
With thy black mantle till strange love grows bold,
Think true love acted simple modesty.

Come, night; come, Romeo; come, thou day in night,
For thou wilt lie upon the wings of night
Whiter than new snow upon a raven's back.
Come, gentle night, come, loving, black-browed night;
Give me my Romeo; and, when he shall die,
Take him and cut him out in little stars,
And he will make the face of heaven so fine
That all the world will be in love with night
And pay no worship to the garish sun.
O, I have bought the mansion of a love,
But not possessed it; and though I am sold,
Not yet enjoyed. So tedious is this day
As is the night before some festival
To an impatient child that hath new robes
And may not wear them.

*Romeo and Juliet* (III.ii)

To die is to be banish'd from myself;
And Silvia is myself: banish'd from her
Is self from self: a deadly banishment!
What light is light, if Silvia be not seen?
What joy is joy if Silvia be not by?
Unless it be to think that she is by
And feed upon the shadow of perfection.
Except I be by Silvia in the night,
There is no music in the nightingale;
Unless I look on Silvia in the day,
There is no day for me to look upon;
She is my essence, and I leave to be,
If I be not by her fair influence
Foster'd, illuminated, cherished, kept alive.
I fly not death, to fly his deadly doom:
Tarry I here, I but attend on death:
But, fly I hence, I fly away from life.

*The Two Gentleman of Verona* (III.i)

To be in love, where scorn is bought with groans;
Coy looks with heart-sore sighs; one fading moments mirth
With twenty watchful, weary, tedious nights:
If haply won, perhaps a hapless gain;
If lost, why then a grievous labour won;
However, but a folly bought with wit,
Or else a wit by folly vanquished.

*The Two Gentlemen of Verona* (I.i)


If music be the food of love, play on,
Give me excess of it, that, surfeiting,
The appetite may sicken, and so die.
That strain again!  It had a dying fall;
O, it came o'er my ear like the sweet sound
That breathes upon a bank of violets,
Stealing and giving odor.

*Twelfth Night* (I.i)

Men are April when they woo, December
when they wed. Maids are May when they are maids
but the sky changes when they are wives. I will be
more jealous of thee than a Barbary cock-pigeon
over his hen, more clamorous than a parrot against
rain, more newfangled than an ape, more giddy in
my desires than a monkey. I will weep for nothing,
like Diana in the fountain, and I will do that when
you are disposed to be merry; I will laugh like a hyen,
and that when thou art inclined to sleep.

*As You Like It* (IV.i)

# SHAKESPEARE'S
# SONGS

Oh mistress mine! where are you roaming?
O, stay and hear; your true love's coming,
    That can sing both high and low.
Trip no further, pretty sweeting;
Journeys end in lovers meeting,
    Every wise man's son doth know.

What is love? 'tis not hereafter;
Present mirth hath present laughter;
    What's to come is still unsure:
In delay there lies no plenty;
Then come kiss me, sweet and twenty,
    Youth's a stuff will not endure.

*Twelfth Night* (II.iii)

Who is Sylvia? What is she,
    That all our swains commend her?
Holy, fair, and wise is she;
    The heaven such grace did lend her,
That she might admired be.

Is she kind as she is fair?
    For beauty lives with kindness.
Love doth to her eyes repair,
    To help him of his blindness,
And, being helped, inhabits there.

Then to Silvia let us sing,
    That Silvia is excelling.
She excels each mortal thing
    Upon the dull earth dwelling;
To her let us garlands bring.

*The Two Gentlemen of Verona* (IV.ii)

Sigh no more, ladies, sigh no more!
    Men were deceivers ever,
One foot in sea, and one on shore;
    To one thing constant never.
Then sigh not so, but let them go,
    And be you blithe and bonny,
Converting all your sounds of woe
    Into Hey nonny, nonny.
Sing no more ditties, sing no moe,
    Of dumps so dull and heavy;
The fraud of men was ever so,
    Since summer first was leavy;
        Then sigh not so, &c.

*Much Ado About Nothing* (II.iii)

Take, O take those lips away,

    That so sweetly were forsworn;

And those eyes, the break of day,

    Lights that do mislead the morn;

But my kisses bring again, bring again;

Seals of love, but sealed in vain,

sealed in vain.

*Measure for Measure* (IV.i)

Being it

is but

flatterin

to be su

I am afeard,

Being in night,

all this is but a dream,

Too flattering sweet

to be substantial.

# SHAKESPEARE'S
# SONNETS

# ❧ 18 ❧

Shall I compare thee to a summer's day?
Thou art more lovely and more temperate:
Rough winds do shake the darling buds of May,
And summer's lease hath all too short a date.
Sometime too hot the eye of heaven shines,
And often is his gold complexion dimmed;
And every fair from fair sometime declines,
By chance, or nature's changing course untrimmed;
But thy eternal summer shall not fade,
Nor lose possession of that fair thou ow'st,
Nor shall death brag thou wander'st in his shade,
When in eternal lines to time thou grow'st,
    So long as men can breathe, or eyes can see,
    So long lives this, and this gives life to thee.

## ∞ 23 ∞

As an unperfect actor on the stage,
Who with his fear is put beside his part,
Or some fierce thing replete with too much rage,
Whose strength's abundance weakens his own heart:
So I, for fear of trust, forget to say
The perfect ceremony of love's rite,
And in mine own  love's strength seem to decay,
O'ercharged with burden of mine own love's might.
O, let my books be then the eloquence
And dumb presagers of my speaking breast,
Who plead for love and look for recompense
More than that tongue that more hath more expressed.
   O, learn to read what silent love hath writ:
   To hear with eyes belongs to love's fine wit.

## ❧ 24 ❧

Mine eye hath played the painter and hath steeled
Thy beauty's form in table of my heart;
My body is the frame wherein 'tis held.
And perspective it is best painter's art,
For through the painter must you see his skill,
To find where your true image pictured lies,
Which in my bosom's shop is hanging still,
That hath his windows glazèd with thine eyes.
Now see what good turns eyes for eyes have done:
Mine eyes have drawn thy shape, and thine for me
Are windows to my breast, wherethrough the sun
Delights to peep, to gaze therein on thee.
 Yet eyes this cunning want to grace their art,
 They draw but what they see, know not the heart.

## ❧ 29 ❧

When, in disgrace with Fortune and men's eyes,
I all alone beweep my outcast state,
And trouble deaf heaven with my bootless cries,
And look upon myself, and curse my fate,
Wishing me like to one more rich in hope,
Featured like him, like him with friends possessed,
Desiring this man's art and that man's scope,
With what I most enjoy contented least:
Yet in these thoughts myself almost despising,
Haply I think on thee, and then my state,
Like to the lark at break of day arising
From sullen earth, sings hymns at heaven's gate;
    For thy sweet love remembered such wealth brings
    That then I scorn to change my state with kings.

## ❧ 40 ❧

Take all my loves, my love, yea, take them all:
What hast thou then more than thou hadst before?
No love, my love, that thou mayst true love call;
All mine was thine before thou hadst this more.
Then, if for my love thou my love receivest,
I cannot blame thee for thou my love usest;
But yet be blamed if thou this self deceivest
By willful taste of what thyself refusest.
I do forgive thy robb'ry, gentle thief,
Although thou steal thee all my poverty;
And yet love knows it is a greater grief
To bear love's wrong than hate's known injury.

 Lascivious grace, in whom all ill well shows,
 Kill me with spites; yet we must not be foes.

Mine eye and heart are at a mortal war
How to divide the conquest of thy sight;
Mine eye my heart thy picture's sight would bar,
My heart mine eye the freedom of that right.
My heart doth plead that thou in him dost lie—
A closet never pierced with crystal eyes;
But the defendant doth that plea deny,
And says in him thy fair appearance lies.
To 'cide this title is impanelèd
A quest of thoughts, all tenants to the heart;
And by their verdict is determinèd
The clear eye's moiety, and the dear heart's part:
 As thus—mine eye's due is thy outward part,
 And my heart's right thy inward love of heart.

My only love sprung
from my only hate.
Too early seen unknown,
and known too late.

## ⤳ 49 ⤳

Against that time, if ever that time come,
When I shall see thee frown on my defects,
When as my love hath cast his utmost sum,
Called to that audit by advised respects:
Against that time when thou shalt strangely pass,
And scarcely greet me with that sun, thine eye,
When love, converted from the thing it was,
Shall reasons find of settled gravity.
Against that time do I esconce me here
Within the knowledge of mine own desert,
And this my hand against myself uprear,
To guard the lawful reasons on thy part:
    To leave poor me thou hast the strength of laws,
    Since why to love I can allege no cause.

## ∞ 57 ∞

*B*eing your slave, what should I do but tend
Upon the hours and times of your desire?
I have no precious time at all to spend,
Nor services to do, till you require.
Nor dare I chide the world-without-end hour
Whilst I, my sovereign, watch the clock for you,
Nor think the bitterness of absence sour
When you have bid your servant once adieu.
Nor dare I question with my jealous thought
Where you may be, or your affairs suppose,
But like a sad slave stay and think of nought
Save, where you are, how happy you make those.
    So true a fool is love that in your will,
    Though you do anything, he thinks no ill.

## ∽ 71 ∽

No longer mourn for me when I am dead
Then you shall hear the surly sullen bell
Give warning to the world that I am fled
From this vile world with vilest worms to dwell:
Nay, if you read this line, remember not
The hand that writ it, for I love you so
That I  in your sweet thoughts would be forgot
If thinking on me then should make you woe.
O if, I say, you look upon this verse
When I  perhaps compounded am with clay,
Do not so much as my poor name rehearse,
But let your love even with my life decay:
    Lest the wise world should look into your moan,
    And mock you with me after I am gone.

## ❦ 86 ❦

Was it the proud full sail of his great verse,
Bound for the prize of all too precious you,
That did my ripe thoughts in my brain inhearse,
Making their tomb the womb wherein they grew?
Was it his spirit, by spirits taught to write
Above a mortal pitch, that struck me dead?
No, neither he, nor his compeers by night
Giving him aid, my verse astonished.
He, nor that affable familiar ghost
Which nightly gulls him intelligence,
As victors of my silence cannot boast:
I was not sick of any fear from thence.
　　But when your countenance filled up his line,
　　Then lacked I matter : that enfeebled mine.

## ❧ 98 ❧

From you have I been absent in the spring,
When proud-pied April, dressed in all his trim,
Hath put a spirit of youth in everything,
That heavy Saturn laughed and leaped with him,
Yet nor the lays of birds, nor the sweet smell
Of different flowers in odor and in hue,
Could make me any summer's story tell,
Or from their proud lap pluck them where they grew.
Nor did I wonder at the lily's white,
Nor praise the deep vermilion in the rose;
They were but sweet, but figures of delight,
Drawn after you, you pattern of all those.
      Yet seemed it winter still, and, you away,
      As with your shadow I with these did play.

## ❧ 104 ❧

To me, fair friend, you never can be old,
For as you were when first your eye I eyed,
Such seems your beauty still: three winters cold
Have from the forests shook three summers' pride,
Three beauteous springs to yellow autumn turned
In process of the seasons have I seen,
Three April perfumes in three hot Junes burned,
Since first I saw you fresh, which yet are green.
Ah, yet doth beauty like a dial-hand
Steal from his figure, and no pace perceived;
So your sweet hue, which methinks still doth stand,
Hath motion, and mine eye may be deceived:
    For fear of which, hear this, thou age unbred:
    Ere you were born was beauty's summer dead.

When in the chronicle of wasted time
I see descriptions of the fairest wights,
And beauty making beautiful old rhyme
In praise of ladies dead and lovely knights;
Then, in the blazon of sweet beauty's best,
Of hand, of foot, of lip, of eye, of brow,
I see their antique pen would have expressed
Even such a beauty as you master now.
So all their praises are but prophecies
Of this our time, all you prefiguring,
And, for they looked but with divining eyes,
They had not still enough your worth to sing:
    For we, which now behold these present days,
    Have eyes to wonder, but lack tongues to praise.

My boun

oundless

My love

the    more

The    more

My bounty is as
boundless as the sea,
My love as deep:the more I
give to thee
The more I have,
for both are infinite.

## ❧ 116 ❧

Let me not to the marriage of true minds
Admit impediments; love is not love
Which alters when it alteration finds
Or bends with the remover to remove.
O, no, it is an ever-fixed mark
That looks on tempests and is never shaken;
It is the star to every wand'ring bark,
Whose worth's unknown, although his height be taken.
Love's not Time's fool, though rosy lips and cheeks
Within his bending sickle's compass come;
Love alters not with his brief hours and weeks,
But bears it out even to the edge of doom.
    If this be error, and upon me proved,
    I never writ, nor no man ever loved.

## ⟩ 130 ⟨

My mistress' eyes are nothing like the sun;
Coral is far more red than her lips' red.
If snow be white, why then her breasts are dun;
If hairs be wires, black wires grow on her head.
I have seen roses damasked, red and white,
But no such roses see I in her cheeks;
And in some perfumes is there more delight
Than in the breath that from my mistress reeks.
I love to hear her speak; yet well I know
That music hath a far more pleasing sound.
I grant I never saw a goddess go;
My mistress, when she walks, treads on the ground.
    And yet, by heaven, I think my love as rare
    As any she belied with false compare.

## ∽ 138 ∽

When my love swears that she is made of truth
I do believe her, though I know she lies,
That she might think me some untutored youth,
Unlearned in the world's false subtleties.
Thus vainly thinking that she thinks me young,
Although she knows my days are past the best,
Simply I credit her false-speaking tongue;
On both sides thus is simple truth suppressed.
But wherefore says she not she is unjust?
And wherefore say not I that I am old?
O, love's best habit is in seeming trust,
And age in love loves not to have years told.
  Therefore I lie with her and she with me,
  And in our faults by lies we flattered be.

# ⟨∾ About Shakespeare ∾⟩

William Shakespeare was born in April 1564 in Stratford-upon-Avon, England, the eldest of four boys and two girls born to John Shakespeare, a trader and prominent local politician, and Mary Arden, the daughter of a landowner. In 1582, at the age of eighteen, Shakespeare married Ann Hathaway, who was eight years his senior. Their daughter, Susanna, was born in 1583, followed by twins, Hamnet and Judith, in 1585.

Little is known about the next few years other than that he spent some time establishing himself as an actor and that by 1592 he had succeeded to prominence in London as both an actor and a writer. In 1594, Shakespeare became a charter member of the Chamberlain's Men, the theater company which later changed its name to the King's Men and included the famous clown, Will Kempe, and actor Richard Burbage. Shakespeare remained with this stable company until his retirement around 1611. After 1599, the King's Men acted primarily in The Globe, a theater in which Shakespeare held a one-tenth interest.

The plague closed London theaters often in the years 1592–1594. During this time Shakespeare published the narrative poems *Venus and Adonis* and *The Rape of*

*Lucrece* and he also began composing his sonnets. These sonnets eventually came to number 154 and were published in 1609. Like the plays, they retain a remarkable universality of themes expressed in metaphorically rich language.

The sonnets were Shakespeare's contribution to a popular poetic form of the times. Aside from them, however, after 1594, Shakespeare turned all his literary efforts to the stage. In all, he is known to have written 37 plays. He completed an average of two plays a year, including *The Two Gentlemen of Verona* by 1595; *Romeo and Juliet* by 1596, *Much Ado About Nothing*, *As You Like It*, and *Twelfth Night* by 1600; and *Measure For Measure* by 1605.

On April 25, 1616, Shakespeare was buried within the chancel of the same church in Stratford where he was christened. Above the grave are the lines, perhaps by the man himself:

Good friend, for Jesus' sake forbear
To dig the dust enclosed here.
Blessed be the man that spares these stones
And cursed be he that moves my bones.

Good night, good night.
Parting is such sweet sorrow
That I shall say good night
till it be morrow.